3

Red Squirrel

sees some nuts.

He eats a big nut.

Red Squirrel
hides some nuts

Story by Beverley Randell   Illustrations by Isabel Lowe

Red Squirrel

is coming down the tree.

He is hungry.

He is going to look

for nuts to eat.

Red Squirrel
is going to hide some nuts.
He runs back to the tree
with a nut.

Red Squirrel
hides the nut.

Look!

Snow is coming down.

Red Squirrel runs up the tree.

He is running home.

Red Squirrel
goes to sleep
inside his home
in the tree.

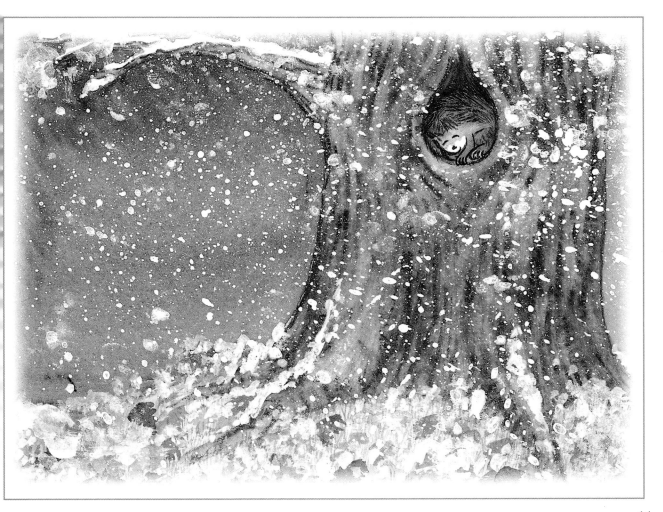

Here comes the sun.

Red Squirrel wakes up.

He is hungry.

He looks down

at the snow.

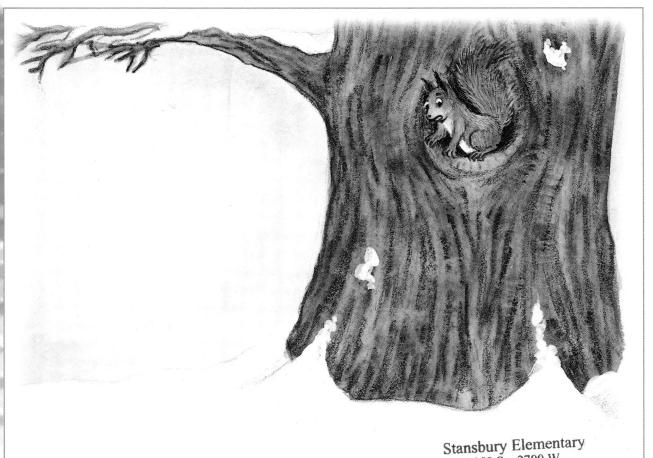

Stansbury Elementary
3050 So. 2700 W.
West Valley City, UT 84119

Red Squirrel comes down.

He can not see a nut to eat.

Where are the nuts?

Where is Red Squirrel going?

Red Squirrel

finds a big nut.

It is down here.

Clever Red Squirrel!